ALIENS STOLE BUSH'S BRAIN

101 REASONS WHY NONE OF THIS IS BUSH'S FAULT

BOOKS BY DOUGLAS WATSON

The Federal Bureau of Alternate Reality
The Federal Bureau of Paperwork Reduction

Darkhaven
Ghosts of Darkhaven

ALIENS STOLE BUSH'S BRAIN

101 REASONS WHY NONE OF THIS IS BUSH'S FAULT

DOUGLAS WATSON

TWIN STAR BOOKS
Portland, Oregon

Copyright © 2005 by Douglas Watson

All rights reserved. No part of this publication may be reproduced, stored in or introduced into a retrieval system, or transmitted, in any form or by any means, without the prior written permission of the copyright owner, except as provided by the U.S. Copyright Law.

All of the symposium participants portrayed in this book are fictitious. Any resemblance between them and actual persons, living or dead, is entirely coincidental.

Cover art by Lynn Pass

ISBN: 978-0-9725046-4-5 / 0-9725046-4-8

First Edition

Printed in the U.S.A.

for Bill and Hillary Clinton,
with thanks for a wonderful eight years

and, of course, for George W. Bush,
without whom none of this would have been possible

let alone his fault

SELECTIONS FROM THE NATIONAL SYMPOSIUM
"THE NATURE AND MEANING OF GEORGE W. BUSH"

1. **DOES BUSH EXIST?** 1
   INTRODUCTORY REMARKS BY THE SYMPOSIUM CHAIR
   Marian Rutherford, Ph.D., Professor of Philosophy, U.C. Berkeley

2. **OOPS, HE DID IT AGAIN** 4
   GEORGE W. BUSH, POP CULTURE ICON
   Erin McKenzie, Student Body President, Ridgecrest High School, White Plains, NY

3. **TAKE OUR PRESIDENT ... PLEASE!** 10
   Jo-Jo Lennux, Comedian

4. **THE DIVINE MISUNDERESTIMATIONS** 17
   A TAOIST-FREUDIAN-EVANGELICAL INTERPRETATION
   OF THE MASTER'S OWN WORDS
   Dr. Lao Ji-Yan, Beijing
   Herr Dr. Zigmund Hoffmeier, Stuttgart
   Rev. Lazarus Tulley, Atlanta

5. **ALIENS STOLE BUSH'S BRAIN** 29
   101 REASONS WHY NONE OF THIS IS BUSH'S FAULT
   Art Lavinsky, Bureau of Internal Affairs, Washington, D.C.

6. **SPRINGTIME FOR BÜSHLER** 37
   A WHITE HOUSE IMPOSTOR REINVENTS THE BIG LIE PRINCIPLE
   Emily Robertson-Santiago, American Civil Liberties Union

7. **THANK GOD THINGS ARE FINALLY LOOKING UP** .. 53
   WHY GEORGE W. BUSH WAS EXACTLY WHAT AMERICA NEEDED
   William L. Thayer IV, President and CEO, Texas Armaments

8. **GEORGE W. BUSH:**
   MYTH, MONSTER, OR MARIONETTE? 59
   CONCLUDING REMARKS BY THE SYMPOSIUM CHAIR
   Marian Rutherford, Ph.D., Professor of Philosophy, U.C. Berkeley

1

DOES BUSH EXIST?
Introductory Remarks by the Symposium Chair

Marian Rutherford, Ph.D., Professor of Philosophy, U.C. Berkeley

Good afternoon, and welcome to the National Symposium on the nature and meaning of George W. Bush. I'm pleased to announce that we have a variety of distinguished speakers here today, from different walks of life, to present a broad spectrum of views on this enigmatic and controversial topic. It falls to me, as symposium chair, to offer a few brief introductory remarks, and then the symposium can begin.

In order to conduct a legitimate symposium on the nature and meaning of George W. Bush, we must first pose the question, "Does Bush exist?"

The philosopher René Descartes famously remarked: "I think, therefore I am." At first glance, that assertion would seem to rule Bush out altogether, as far as any question of existence is concerned. Closer scrutiny of Descartes' statement, however, reveals that thinking is merely a *possible consequence* of existence, not a precondition. Lime Jell-O®, for instance, does not think; yet it exists. A similar line of reasoning may be applicable in the case of George W. Bush.

Scientists and theologians, over the years, have wrestled with similar questions of existence. No scientist, for example, has ever directly observed a black hole; yet scientists are able to postulate the existence of black holes by noting the chaos wreaked upon their surroundings – the gravitational "sinkhole effect" on nearby galaxies, the distortion of galactic patterns, the outpouring of lethal radiation.

Perhaps, then, we may follow a similar logical path to determine the possible existence of George W. Bush. To conduct such an inquiry, we must examine changes known to have taken place around the time when the purported "Bush presidency" is believed to have originated.

Consider, first of all, the attempt to balance the federal budget. From January 1993 to January 2001, during the last "known" presidency – that of William J. Clinton – the federal deficit was reduced systematically each year, resulting in a record budget surplus. After Clinton's departure, that surplus quickly evaporated, and the deficit has expanded at unprecedented rates. Some disturbance in the trend of federal economic policy has evidently taken place. Observable changes in other federal policies – military, environmental, and so forth – have also occurred since Clinton left office.

Whether or not we may attribute these changes directly to the existence of George W. Bush remains to be seen. This is especially true since we have yet to determine precisely what we mean by "Bush." To Democrats, Bush may indeed seem like a black hole; to many Republicans, on the other hand, he seems more like a god. Perhaps, then, we should turn next to theology to gain further insight into the enigma of George W. Bush's existence.

It has been claimed – though we still await independent confirmation – that God has spoken to George W. Bush. This, if verifiable, would certainly provide compelling evidence for the existence of God. The evidence regarding Bush is less conclusive, since being spoken to is not, in itself, a prerequisite for existence. God might have spoken rhetorically, or to some undefined and possibly non-existent entity. However, separate claims have also arisen that Bush has spoken to God. Here, paradoxically, we find ourselves in the opposite predicament: while appearing to support the existence of Bush, these claims fail to substantiate the existence of

God. What we have on our hands is a circular argument. If we could verify, once and for all, a *dialogue* between God and Bush, we could lay to rest any doubt concerning the existence of either of these two phenomena.

In the absence of such verification, however, we must look deeper into the source material: the Bible itself. References here to God are, of course, plentiful; however, references to Bush in the same text are, one must admit, considerably scarcer. Among the more prominent mentions is that of a "burning Bush" – and, as we see, the close association of this Bush with the "voice of God" does indeed provide evidence of a possible God-Bush connection.

We are still left, however, with the fact that we have yet to establish which of the many – and contradictory – "George W. Bushes" we are referring to. Is he a "uniter," or a "divider"? Would a "compassionate conservative" care nothing about outsourced jobs and unaffordable health care, while creating billions in tax breaks for the world's wealthiest individuals? Yet, perhaps, when viewed through the correct lens, such apparent contradictions are not contradictions at all. It may be argued, for instance, that the three-in-one nature of the Trinity offers a theological precedent for Bush's multiple personae. Nor need we confine our exploration to the realm of theology. Science, too, provides numerous examples, as we may observe from the changing and contradictory behavior of subatomic particles in quantum physics. As Nobel Prizewinning physicist Werner Heisenberg noted in his Uncertainty Principle of 1927: "The more precisely the position is determined, the less precisely the momentum is known in this instant." The same may be said of Bush's politics.

I acknowledge that the foregoing remarks may not provide irrefutable proof for the existence of Bush; however, I believe we have sufficient evidence to generate at least a satisfactory working hypothesis. Let the Bush Symposium begin!

2

OOPS, HE DID IT AGAIN
George W. Bush, Pop Culture Icon

Erin McKenzie, Student Body President, Ridgecrest High School, White Plains, NY

Wow. This place sure looks big. Especially from up here. I mean, it's *way* bigger than our high school auditorium, back home in White Plains. It's like … totally huge. But anyway. Luckily, I'm used to this kind of thing, as your student body president. Well, not *your* student body president, of course. Sorry, I'm still a little nervous. I mean, as student body president of Ridgecrest High School, I'm totally used to public speaking, and whatever. So, not a problem.

Well, anyway. It's great to be here. I'm here tonight to talk about our president, George W. Bush, and how he became America's number one pop culture icon.

As you probably know, George W. Bush was first elected president in the year 2000. Well, except that not everyone agrees he was elected. So I guess we should say: in November of the year 2000, Bush defeated Al Gore in the popular vote by … although, actually, Al Gore won the popular vote. Well, but anyway, let's just say George W. Bush made it through to, like, the final round, which was the Supreme Court. And this time Bush ended up winning the popular vote in the Supreme Court, by 5-4, so that meant he became president.

They also had a whole lot of earlier rounds, which I didn't mention, like the primaries and the conventions and stuff like that, where people got voted off. Like they do on "Survivor." In fact, it would be really cool to have a reality show called "Election Survivor," about people running for president, or whatever. Then George W. Bush could be on it. He'd be so cool! He'd be like that guy on "Jeopardy!" where he won like 700 weeks in a row, or something. Can you imagine? It would be totally awesome.

So, anyway, then they had the 2004 election, and George W. Bush was allowed to compete again. Kind of like on "The Bachelorette," where the same person was the Bachelorette twice in a row. So this time George W. Bush won again, so now he's like the champion, and he probably got a new car, and stuff like that. But anyway, so the way he won this time around was to go around to all these churches and register everyone to vote Republican. I know some people were saying it went against the Constitution, because of some kind of Church and State thing, so it was like cheating, or whatever. I mean, come on. The people who said that were just sore losers. It's like saying, "Don't cheat on your term papers," or something. I mean, everybody does it, so why should the president have to be any different? And another way George W. Bush won was by having only rich people come and hear his speeches, and by locking the door against any poor people who tried to get in. But I don't see what's to complain about there, either. Because it's the rich people who have way the most money to give to his campaign. Like: *Duh!* So all of those poor people would just be taking up valuable space, as far as George W. Bush was concerned. It totally makes sense, if you think about it.

I mean, it's pretty much the same way I got elected student body president. You just go around to all of the rich kids and the popular cliques, and find out the kinds of things they want to hear, and then those are the things you say. You don't have to worry too much about the unpopular kids and the kids who don't have any money, because they can't really bring you in a whole lot of votes, or help out with balloons and glitter and stuff for your campaign. So that's just what you have to do, if you want to get elected.

So what is it that makes George W. Bush such a pop culture icon? Well, first of all, it's just the fact that he won. Because everybody loves a winner. You know, like in the song. So, now that George W. Bush is a winner, that means everybody loves him, too. Although I guess not *everybody* loves George W. Bush. In fact, even here in America, there's a whole lot of people who totally don't like him at all. In fact … well, but, anyway. You get the idea of what I'm saying.

Way more important than loving a winner, though, is the fact that everyone always loves a villain. It's like in *Star Wars*. I mean, practically everyone thinks Darth Vader is, like, *way* cooler than Luke Skywalker. Especially now it turns out he's really Hayden Christensen. So the fact that George W. Bush does a lot of super-mean things, like taking people's tax money that they've put in for Social Security, and giving it all to his super-rich friends, actually helps his popularity. Kind of like with Simon on "American Idol," where he always acts totally mean to everyone, but people still like to watch him. Or like on "The Weakest Link." I mean, if George W. Bush could be the host of "The Weakest Link" for a special NATO episode, and say things like "You are the Weakest Link!" to, like, French people and whatever, he'd probably be, like, even more popular than he already is.

One other huge reason why George W. Bush is such a pop culture icon is that he's a totally awesome liar. I mean, lying is like a total turn-on for most people. It's like, when some guy in high school asks you to go out with him, and he says how he loves you, and how he wants what's best for you, and he won't ever cheat on you, and stuff like that, you know? So, even though you kind of know he's lying, you still end up going out with him. It's the same reason people voted for George W. Bush. In America, people don't really appreciate having to hear the truth. Like with the Dixie Chicks.

And another thing. George W. Bush is one totally macho mega-stud for leading us into war against all these other countries. I mean, I know it's other people's kids he's sending off, and not his own, but still. It's the thought that counts. I've heard people complain that this war is really all about oil, but those people don't seem to realize that oil is important. After all, America has a lot more cars than other countries – and a lot more malls to visit, too. So naturally we need a lot more oil than those other places. It makes total sense. Supply and demand. Like in economics class. (See, Mr. Collins? I *was* paying attention! I mean, I so deserved better than a C-minus in that class!) Besides, oil has a whole lot more uses than just cars. It powers all kinds of things. It's like in *Monsters, Inc.*, where the monsters use the screams of the children to power their factories, so they have to make sure they keep up the supply. It's kind of the same idea here, only with oil.

Also, this way, the president can learn all about geography, and where other countries are, and stuff like that. Those are all useful facts for a U.S. President to be aware of. Especially in case he ever needs a foreign policy.

Another reason George W. Bush is so popular is his whole message about morality. Like keeping gay marriage from taking over. I mean, if you're thinking about marrying some guy, it's important to know he isn't going to end up being gay, or whatever. It makes total sense. And I majorly agree with President Bush about changing the Constitution. Most of that stuff in the Constitution is really, *really* old by now. Like from before I was even *born*. I mean, some of those Amendments date all the way back to like Franklin D. Roosevelt, or something. We totally need some more up-to-date issues. Besides, about two-thirds of Americans agree with banning gay marriage, so that shows it's way popular. It'd be, like, "We, the People," that kind of thing. So it would totally tie into democracy, and our nation's history, except now it would be covered on the national news. How cool is that? It would be like having Mt. St. Helens erupt again, only without all of the ash going everywhere.

Which brings me to the environment. I've heard some people complain that President Bush doesn't really do a whole lot for the environment. I guess it would be kind of like in our school, when we have one of those bogus assemblies where we have to clean up the school by going around picking up litter, and whatever. But, if you're the president, why would you have to do that? It seems to me that's why you have servants.

Another reason George W. Bush is a pop culture icon is that his whole entire family is so cool. Take the twins, for example. Those girls really know how to accessorize. You know: the shoes, and stuff. And the hair. Although they could consider taking it a little further once in a while. Maybe more of a Brittney Spears look. You know: like, "Oops, I did it again"? That kind of thing. I could totally see it. Especially for Jenna. For Barbara, maybe more of a Madonna statement. Or I bet she could lip-synch awesomely. She could start out as maybe Ashlee Simpson, and like work her way up. Hard to tell. I'd have to see it. But, like, those girls really rock.

And then Laura. I mean, she's such a total role model. She's like so all-American, and totally supportive of her husband, and everything. She probably even bakes her own brownies. Seriously: can you see Laura Bush going on to become a U.S. Senator, like Hillary Clinton? No way. There is *no way*. I mean, read my lips: "No way." And Laura has, like, totally killer dress sense, too. Those kinds of things are important in a First Lady.

And did you know – Laura Bush was once a librarian? So she really knows books. Which makes kind of a useful division of labor with the president, since he doesn't know all that much about reading. But I think it's so cool that the president really cares about education for others. Like, he came up with the whole idea of No Child Left Behind. I bet he wishes something like that had been around when he was in school. That would probably really help him out now, as president. But then, he should maybe have gone to our school, in White Plains. We have a whole program about helping kids learn to read. Too bad the program's getting cut under No Child Left Behind. But I understand there are lots of other priorities for our education money, like the war in Iraq. I realize how important it is to bomb schools in other countries, so their kids won't get ahead of us. That way, America can stay number one.

So, altogether, George W. Bush is like, totally, the coolest president ever! And the way he grins like a monkey is just the best! Who cares if he doesn't know anything? It's only for eight years, and then we can go back to having some boring president who worries about the economy, and stuff like that. By then, I'll be thinking about graduating from college and looking for a job, so the timing will work out just great.

Meanwhile, I say: "Party on, America!"

While we still have a country left.

3
TAKE OUR PRESIDENT ... PLEASE!

Jo-Jo Lennux, Comedian

It's great to see so many of you here this evening. No, really. The last place I played was the Donald Rumsfeld Fan Club. Half of the seats were empty. Literally. One of their two members couldn't make it that night.

No, but seriously. Rumsfeld was great about it. He told me not to worry. He said: "Just play to the fan I have, not the fans I'd like to have."

But let me tell you, it's not easy to have friends these days. Especially in politics. Take George W. Bush, for instance. Did you know George W. was friends with God? Sure. They talk all the time. Great friends. Or they used to be. That was before Bush told God: "You're either with me, or against me."

So, later on, Bush tries to make it up to God. He says: "Listen. I'll tell you what I'll do. I'll ban the teaching of evolution in our public schools. It'll be just Creationism from now on." And God says: "You're kidding." He says: "You're kidding me, right? I mean, any deity can put a planet together in six days. I spent billions of years on evolution! And now you're not even going to teach it?"

Like I said, it's tough to have friends in politics. You just can't please everyone.

So, anyway, George W. Bush dies, and he goes up to heaven, and he's met at the gate by St. Peter. And St. Peter says to him, "Now, before you come in, George, you have to make a choice. We offer this same choice to everyone. You have to decide: Do you want the Classic Heaven, or the Compassionate Conservative Heaven?"

So George W. thinks about that for a moment. He flips through a couple of brochures. And he thinks to himself: Well, the Classic Heaven does sound pretty good. On the other hand, I *am* George W. Bush. How would it look to everyone else if I didn't pick the Compassionate Conservative Heaven? Besides, the Compassionate Conservative Heaven has all of the things I worked so hard in life to achieve: no freedom of speech, no free press, no protection against search and seizure, no gay marriage, no death with dignity, no environmental pollution restrictions … it's going to be great. So he turns to St. Peter and says, "All right. I'll take the Compassionate Conservative Heaven."

And St. Peter says, "Well, that's fine, George. The only thing is, you'll have to bring your own food. We're not going to cook for just one person."

Like I say, it's tough to please everyone.

No, really. You think it's easy being president? Think about everything Bush has to do.

The neo-Conservative agenda, for example. I mean, how in the world does one guy come up with all that stuff?

I tell you, something like that must take a whole lot of sitting around in the Oval Office, waiting for inspiration.

So he gathers his aides around him, and starts work. It takes him a moment to get warmed up. Then he gets a big one. "Say. Here's an idea. Tax giveaways for the rich. Hey, and then those grateful rich can pay a nice chunk right back in the form of presidential campaign contributions. It's a win-win situation for everyone! Well, except for the rest of America, of course. But they don't really count."

And everyone else is going: "Yes, sir." "Great idea, sir." "Sounds wonderful, sir."

So now Bush is really hitting his stride. He leans back in his chair a little. "And let's see. Jobs. Unemployment's just great for business, because if jobs are scarce those greedy workers will be glad to get anything, so they'll work for peanuts. Better start Operation Outsource America right away."

"Oh, yes, sir." "Sounds great, sir." "Terrific plan, sir."

"Let's see. And what else? A war, maybe ..." I mean, is there no *stopping* this guy? "Yes – a war would benefit most of the people I know: the munitions companies ... Halliburton ... even the oil industry, if we pick the right country to invade. It'll cost a couple of billion a week, but that's just taxpayer money. Nothing you rich folks have to worry about ..."

So, next he has to sell all of this to the rest of the country. And keep a straight face at the same time. Now, you're probably thinking, that's not going to be easy.

Well, for most presidents, maybe not.

But, you see, that's where Bush is smart. No, really. He is. George W. Bush made the smartest move any president ever made. He picked Dick Cheney as his vice president.

Think about that. Dick Cheney, next in line for the White House. You think anyone's going to impeach Bush? The guy can get away with anything he likes!

Imagine. *President Cheney.* Now, there are two words that don't belong together in the English language. Not outside of a Stephen King novel, anyway.

It's like this guy who's driving along in Washington, D.C., and he really can't stand the whole Bush-Cheney crowd. Especially Dick Cheney. So every time he sees someone walking along the street who's connected in any way with the Bush Administration, he pulls hard on the steering wheel, and swerves his car up on to the sidewalk, and runs the person down with that satisfying *klunk*, and then he swerves back on to the road, and keeps going.

So he's driving along, keeping one eye out for Bush Republicans, when he sees this priest at the side of the road, thumbing a lift. So he thinks: Well, I'd better give this guy a ride. So he pulls over, and leans across and opens the door, and says, "How far are you going?" And the priest says, "Just to the Church, about a mile down the street." So the guy says, "Hop in, Father. I'll take you there." So the priest gets in, and fastens his seat belt, and off they go.

Well, they hadn't gone but a couple of blocks, when the guy sees Dick Cheney walking along the sidewalk. And he thinks to himself: Man, this is the chance of a lifetime! So he pulls hard on the steering wheel, and swerves up on to the sidewalk, and he's just about to hit Dick Cheney, when he suddenly realizes: What am I doing?! I've got a man of the cloth sitting right here in the car next to me! I can't run over the vice president! So, just in the nick of time, he pulls back hard the other way on the steering wheel, and he swerves the car back out on to the road. But he still hears that familiar *klunk*.

So he turns to the priest and says, "I can't think what happened back there, Father! I'm absolutely positive I swerved in time to avoid hitting him. There's no way I could have run over Dick Cheney." And the priest says, "Don't worry, my son. I got him with the door."

Yup. It's nice to have someone help you out once in a while, isn't it? Of course, Bush has it easy the same way. Other people do everything for him. What a life! He doesn't need to do a thing. He didn't even have to steal his own election. All taken care of.

And speaking of elections – how about that Viktor Yushchenko, in Ukraine? Hey? Let's give it up for the Orange Revolution!

Ah, yes. Remember when America had the credibility to insist on free and fair elections overseas? Well, thanks to Bush, those days are gone. Democracy has become an international free-for-all. Uh-huh. Within two or three weeks of Bush's reelection, widespread allegations of voter fraud began surfacing in Ukraine. And get this – the Bush Administration actually had the *chutzpah* to lead the charge in condemning Yanukovych for stealing the election. ("Hello?? Who raised the bar in election fraud?")

At least, over there in Ukraine, they got it together to hold a revote. Not like here. Luckily, those Ukrainians know a thing or two about democracy. Can you imagine 200,000 protesters in the streets of Kiev being fobbed off with some story about "hanging chad"?

So, Bush didn't have to worry too much about getting elected. That's for other people to deal with. Like the Supreme Court.

Still, being president has to make a person stop and think. Even George W. Bush. And he must be wondering: What would it feel like to do something all by myself, once in a while?

Like the time when George W. Bush was sitting in the back of his limousine, being driven along Pennsylvania Avenue, when he starts thinking to himself: I wonder what it would be like to drive one of these limousines? So he switches on the microphone, and he says to the driver, "What's it like, driving a limousine?" And the driver says, "It's all right, sir. I kind of enjoy it." So Bush switches off the microphone again.

But pretty soon he starts thinking: You know, I'd really like to give it a try. So he switches on the microphone again, and says to the driver, "Why don't you pull over? I'd like to try driving for a while." And the driver says, "I don't think that would be such a good idea, Mr. President. Just sit back and relax, sir. I'm sure you have a lot of important matters of state to think about." So Bush switches the microphone back off. And he knows he doesn't really spend much time thinking about important matters of state, but he's glad, as president, that at least he still has that kind of reputation among his staff.

But then he starts thinking about driving the limousine again. And this time the idea just won't let go of him. So he switches on the microphone again, and he says, "Driver, I'd like you to pull over. I want to try driving this limousine." And the driver thinks to himself: Well, after all, this guy *is* the president. What am I supposed to say? So he pulls over, and he gets out of the car, and George W. Bush gets in the driver's seat, and the driver gets in the back.

Well, no sooner is George W. Bush behind the wheel of that limousine, than he floors the gas pedal and roars out into the traffic, weaving from one lane to another, tires screeching. And he hasn't gone more than a couple of blocks, when he sees those red and blue lights in his rear-view mirror, and a cop pulls him over. So the cop gets out of the patrol car, and walks over, and George W. Bush rolls down the window. And the cop takes a look inside, and he says, "Wait just a minute. I'll be right back."

So the cop goes back to his patrol car, and calls over to his sergeant, and he says, "I just pulled this guy over, but I've got a problem." And the sergeant says, "What kind of problem?" So the cop says, "Well, we're definitely talking VIP here." And the sergeant says, "Look, we got all kinds of VIPs in Washington. Is this guy a Congressman, or what?" And the cop says, "No, no. Bigger than that." And the sergeant says, "A Senator?" And the cop says, "Much worse. This guy's definitely a top-ranking VIP." So the sergeant says, "Well ... a Supreme Court Justice, then? Who *is* this guy?" And the cop says, "Well, that's the thing. I've never seen him before in my life. But let's put it this way. George W. Bush is his driver."

So, as you can see, things could be worse. We could actually have George W. Bush running the country, instead of a bunch of guys like Karl Rove.

Of course, those guys were never elected to the office of president. But then, if we worried about technicalities like that, we'd have Al Gore.

Still, I'll say one thing for Bush. He's made stupidity an art form. No, really. Look on the bright side. We may not have the Theory of Evolution in our school curriculum, but at least *My Pet Goat* is required reading.

But stupidity is really "in" these days. It's finally cool to be dumb. In fact, it's caught on so successfully that Bush has even come up with a new education policy. He's calling it "No Child Left Ahead."

So, anyway, St. Peter is up at the Pearly Gates one day, going about his business, when he looks up and sees this guy ready to come in. So he says to the guy, "Who are you?" And the guy says, "I'm Albert Einstein." And St. Peter says, "Well, OK, but the thing is, anyone can just come along and claim to be Albert Einstein. You'll have to show me some kind of proof." So Einstein looks around, and he says, "Do you mind if I borrow that chalkboard?" And St. Peter says, "Go ahead, be my guest." So Einstein takes the chalkboard, and with a few deft strokes he outlines a pretty good summary of the Theory of Relativity. And he hands the chalkboard back to St. Peter, and St. Peter takes a look at it, and he says: "That's good enough for me, Albert. Come on in!"

So pretty soon another guy comes along, and St. Peter says to him, "Who are you?" And the guy says, "I'm Pablo Picasso." And St. Peter says, "Well, OK, but like I was just telling Albert here, we get all kinds of people coming along claiming to be people they're not. You'll have to show me some kind of proof that you're really Pablo Picasso." So Picasso says, "All right. Do you mind if I borrow that chalkboard?" And St. Peter says, "Go ahead, be my guest." So Picasso takes the chalkboard, and erases it, and then with a few deft strokes he sketches out a pretty good outline of *Guernica*. And he hands the chalkboard back to St. Peter, and St. Peter looks at the chalkboard, and he says: "That's good enough for me, Pablo. Come on in!"

So then this third guy comes along, and St. Peter says, "And who are you?" And the guy says, "I'm George W. Bush." And St. Peter says, "Well, that's fine, but like I was just telling these other two, we sometimes have people trying to get in here under false pretenses. You'll have to show me some kind of proof that you're really George W. Bush." And Bush thinks for a minute, and finally he says, "I can't really think of anything I can do." And St. Peter says, "Well, let me see if I can help you out a little. You could maybe try something along the lines of what your two predecessors did. We just had Albert Einstein and Pablo Picasso." And Bush frowns, and he thinks for a minute, and finally he says, "Well … so, who are they?" And St. Peter says: "That's good enough for me, George. Come on in!"

Thank you. You've been a wonderful audience. Thank you very much, and good night.

4
THE DIVINE MISUNDERESTIMATIONS
A Taoist-Freudian-Evangelical Interpretation
Of The Master's Own Words

Panel:
Dr. Lao Ji-Yan, Beijing
Herr Dr. Zigmund Hoffmeier, Stuttgart
Rev. Lazarus Tulley, Atlanta

Moderator:
Professor Marian Rutherford, Ph.D., Symposium Chair

Rutherford: We come now to the panel discussion segment of today's symposium on the nature and meaning of George W. Bush. Our panelists are Dr. Lao, a noted Taoist scholar from Beijing …

Lao: Greetings.

Rutherford: … Dr. Hoffmeier, a practicing Freudian psychiatrist from Stuttgart …

Hoffmeier: Good evening.

Rutherford: … and the Reverend Tulley, an Evangelical minister from Atlanta.

Tulley: A pleasure to be here.

Rutherford: Welcome, all of you. I'd like to start with a quote which is fundamental to any analysis of the words of George W. Bush. On September 23, 2004, he said: "I think it's very important for the American President to mean what he says. That's why I understand that the enemy could misread what I say. That's why I try to be as clearly I can." Your thoughts? Yes – Dr.

Hoffmeier?

Hoffmeier: I find it revealing that Bush "understands" the tendency to misread. He may perhaps misspeak from his own text; or it may be an unconscious admission, dating back to his childhood, that reading has never come easily to him. He also considers it important to "mean what he says," not to "say what he means," in order to confuse the enemy.

Rutherford: The enemy may not be alone here. Reverend Tulley?

Tulley: When I study this text, I notice those first two words: "I think." The president isn't saying it's important to mean what he says. He says he *thinks* it's important. He *believes*. Regardless of whether he actually means what he says, the point is he believes in the importance. He has faith. And it's this faith that leads him to understand his enemy's weakness.

Rutherford: Interesting. Dr. Lao?

Lao: The Master tells us: "That's why I try to be as clearly I can."

Rutherford: You think perhaps he misspoke here?

Lao: I don't think so. The Master is finding the Way of the Tao. To "speak" clearly, or even to "mean" clearly: these things are fleeting. But to "be" clearly: this is the path every river must take to the sea. Otherwise, what trust can you place in your own self?

Rutherford: Quite so. And, speaking of trust, he said on August 30, 2000: "I think if you say you're going to do something, and don't do it, that's trustworthiness."

Hoffmeier: And I believe he also said, just a few weeks later: "There's a huge trust. I see it all the time when people come up to me and say, 'I don't want you to let me down again.'"

Rutherford: He did. You're absolutely right, Zigi.

Tulley: But, as we know, it's easy to trust those who fulfill their promises. The point here is that the president is asking us to trust him, *despite the fact* that he has let us down in the past.

Lao: Perhaps he asks because of this fact.

Tulley: He says: "There's a huge trust. *I see it all the time.*" So the president is showing us his faith in humanity. He sees trust in others, even those who cannot see it in themselves.

Rutherford: A valid point. Well, turning now to some of George W. Bush's more esoteric statements, he said on September 29, 2000: "I know the human being and fish can coexist peacefully." Dr. Lao, perhaps you can provide some insight here?

Lao: The Tao says: "Just as the fish must not leave the ocean, so the ruler must not display his weapons."

Rutherford: I see … could you perhaps elaborate?

Lao: The Master is saying that, to find the way of peace, the wise ruler learns even from the fish, by keeping to his own domain.

Rutherford: And, evidently, by not displaying his weapons. Dr. Hoffmeier?

Hoffmeier: A little too Freudian, I think, even for me.

Rutherford: Acknowledged. Reverend Tulley?

Tulley: I see a different interpretation here. The fish is intended as a Christian symbol. The president is reassuring America that, even under an Evangelical administration, every person can coexist in peace.

Rutherford: So he's a uniter, not a divider?

Tulley: That would be my interpretation, certainly.

Rutherford: Moving, then, from the esoteric to the paradoxical, he told some VIP visitors to the White House on June 18, 2001: "I'm sure you can imagine it's an unimaginable honor to live here." Dr. Lao – your area of expertise, perhaps?

Lao: The Master is simply affirming that it lies within all of us to imagine the unimaginable, to know the unknowable.

Rutherford: Easier than it sounds, I dare say. Reverend Tulley?

Tulley: He's also reminding us that those who believe in the Afterlife imagine the unimaginable on a daily basis. So, by saying he is "sure" his visitors can do this, the president is stating his belief that they will find eternal salvation.

Rutherford: I see. Good clarification. Now, on September 24, 2001, George W. Bush told the Prime Minister of Canada at the time, Jean Chretien: "Border relations between Canada and Mexico have never been better." Dr. Hoffmeier?

Hoffmeier: I think Mr. Bush, as president, is representing himself here symbolically as America. By referring to border relations between Canada and Mexico, he tells us of his deep anxiety that, at some unconscious level, he himself does not exist. A possibility you explored earlier today, in your introductory remarks.

Rutherford: Indeed. So – a cry for help, then?

Hoffmeier: Very much a cry for help. This is a deep-seated neurosis, again probably originating from his childhood, when he grew up around people more educated than himself.

Rutherford: Is there a connection here, then, with his assertion on August 29, 2002: "There's no cave deep enough for America, or dark enough to hide"?

Hoffmeier: A strong connection, yes. Here, we see that the same neurosis has become more pronounced. He again substitutes himself for America, telling us there is no cave deep enough or dark enough for him to hide in. These are powerful symbols of the unconscious mind. The "cave" is suggesting perhaps a desire to return to the womb; that he wishes, in a sense, that he had never been born.

Rutherford: Reverend Tulley, you look as if you disagree?

Tulley: Yes, I do. I see a more hopeful symbolism in the president's words. Just as the cave where Our Lord was laid after the crucifixion proved neither deep enough nor dark enough to hide His light, so in America's case shall the "fire of freedom" sweep forth across continents, as a beacon for the entire world.

Rutherford: So, this quote signifies freedom?

Tulley: Freedom, definitely. And world peace.

Hoffmeier: Also, that Canada and Mexico still won't have border relations.

Rutherford: Very true. Dr. Lao: "There's no cave deep enough for America, or dark enough to hide." Your thoughts?

Lao: The Master describes the way of the Tao. He is saying: "What is dark, is light; what is hidden, is in plain sight; what is deep, is lifted up."

Rutherford: Yet, at face value, his words don't sound all that optimistic?

Lao: As the Master revealed to us on June 15, 2004: "If you want to try to find something to be pessimistic about, you can find it, no matter how hard you look."

Rutherford: That's right; he did. Can you describe that a little more?

Lao: The Tao tells us: "The harder you look, the less you find." Yet, if you search among the depths, you will find even what you do not seek. This is why the Master also revealed, on September 21, 2003: "I glance at the headlines just to kind of get a flavor for what's moving. I rarely read the stories."

Rutherford: And perhaps why he also said: "I'm the master of low expectations"?

Lao: The Master honors the Tao by seeking the path of humility. He acquaints himself with the glorious, yet keeps to the lowly.

Rutherford: Quite so. Dr. Hoffmeier?

Hoffmeier: I see this as reinforcing the feelings of inferiority I mentioned earlier. His avoidance of reading in any form, combined with his unconscious pessimism-fixation, have created a self-fulfilling prophecy for his own expectations as president.

Tulley: I'm afraid I must disagree again. The text is very clear here. When the president says he is the "master" of low expectations, he means quite literally that he has mastered them. He has risen above them, no doubt as a result of his faith. As he told us back in September, 2000: "One of the common denominators I have found is that expectations rise above that which is expected."

Rutherford: Good point. And, speaking of expectations, one of his most celebrated remarks came after the November 2000 election, when he told supporters: "They misunderestimated me." Your analysis? Yes – Dr. Hoffmeier?

Hoffmeier: I think we need to view this in the context of a statement he made a few months earlier, when he said: "I think anybody who doesn't think I'm smart enough to handle the job is underestimating."

Rutherford: So, here he's using "underestimating" in the literal sense of being something of an understatement?

Hoffmeier: Correct. And then later, when he says, "They misunderestimated me," he's telling us the original level of underestimation was inaccurate. Whether too high or too low, he doesn't specify.

Rutherford: What's your sense of this misunderestimation, Dr. Lao? Too high, or too low?

Lao: This is not for us to speculate. As the Master revealed to us in May of 2000: "I think we agree, the past is over."

Rutherford: And later, of course, he went on to claim: "I understand reality. If you're asking me, as the president, would I understand reality, I do."

Lao: The Wise One understands that the bright path appears dim.

Rutherford: That's certainly one way of putting it. Dr. Hoffmeier, perhaps you can shed some light here? Or provide some insight?

Hoffmeier: Or, as Mr. Bush might say, "shed some insight."

Rutherford: *Touché*, indeed.

Hoffmeier: Well, I think he does understand reality, in one sense. After all, he warned us on September 18, 2000: "America better beware of a candidate who is willing to stretch reality in order to win points."

Rutherford: Fair warning; I agree. Just as when he said: "I want everybody to hear loud and clear that I'm going to be the president of everybody."

Hoffmeier: Exactly so. This is the so-called "Napoleon complex," where a person who feels a sense of inferiority tries to compensate by becoming dictatorial in his dealings with others. Thus he told the nation, on July 27, 2001: "A dictatorship would be a heck of a lot easier, there's no question about it." And he went further on August 9, 2004, when he said: "Let me put it to you bluntly. In a changing world, we want more people to have control over your own life."

Rutherford: Reverend Tulley, you look as if you may disagree again?

Tulley: Yes, I do, very much. That last statement, if we examine the text carefully, is clearly a reflection of the president's Christian viewpoint. He's telling the American people not to carry their burdens alone, but to share the load – the "control," if you will – with more people in their Church community. And, of course, with God Himself.

Rutherford: A useful observation. And perhaps he was sharing his own burden back in June, 2001, when he told Swedish Prime Minister Goran Perrson: "It's amazing I won. I was running against peace, prosperity, and incumbency." Yes – Dr. Hoffmeier?

Hoffmeier: Well, those things are difficult to run against, in any democracy. By 2004, of course, running against incumbency was no longer an option. Yet he still campaigned very actively against peace and prosperity.

Rutherford: And very successfully, too. Which leads us to the war in Iraq. On May 25, 2004, George W. Bush announced in our nation's capital: "I'm honored to shake the hand of a brave Iraqi citizen who had his hand cut off by Saddam Hussein." Anyone care to try that one? Yes – Reverend Tulley?

Tulley: I'm reminded here of the time Our Lord told the lame man at the Pool of Bethesda: "Arise; take up thy bed, and walk." I think the president is saying that, even though he used the U.S. military to wage war against Iraq, he also brings the power to heal. So, in a very real sense, he is extending the healing hand of the Lord to the entire Iraqi people.

Rutherford: And perhaps, in this same spirit of healing, he reassured the world on June 18, 2002: "I just want you to know that, when we talk about war, we're really talking about peace." Dr. Lao?

Lao: Often, when talking of peace, politicians really talk of war. So here the Master shrewdly reminds us that the other way around is also possible. As the Tao says: "Even the mighty war-horses fertilize the fields with their droppings."

Rutherford: An apt metaphor, indeed. Reverend Tulley?

Tulley: I think the president is talking here on a more spiritual level, referring to the war against Satan which we all must wage in order to find eternal peace in God's presence.

Rutherford: Entirely possible. Dr. Hoffmeier?

Hoffmeier: I find it revealing that Mr. Bush begins with the phrase: "I just want you to know …" He never actually claims that, by talking about war, he's really talking about peace. He merely says that he "wants you to know" this.

Rutherford: So was he talking about peace or war, in your opinion, when he said: "The vast majority of Iraqis want to live in a peaceful, free world. And we will find these people, and we will bring them to justice"?

Hoffmeier: This is what we call a "Freudian slip," when the speaker unconsciously reveals his true intentions, despite attempting to conceal them. Perhaps Mr. Bush feels some deep-seated confusion about his motives for the war in Iraq. This would explain why he said: "A free Iraq will be a major defeat in the cause of freedom." And also: "Free nations don't develop weapons of mass destruction."

Rutherford: Or, as he revealingly called them on November 27, 2002: "Weapons of mass production."

Hoffmeier: Exactly so.

Lao: The Master knows that, to defeat our enemies, we must inhabit the thoughts of our enemies. This is why he disclosed to us, on August 5, 2004: "Our enemies are innovative and resourceful, and so are we. They never stop thinking about new ways to harm our country and our people, and neither do we."

Rutherford: An inventive strategy, to be sure. Well, moving from the war to other topics, George W. Bush announced in January, 2000: "The most important job is not to be governor, or first lady in my case." Dr. Hoffmeier, you might take that one?

Hoffmeier: The first point is his rejection of self, when he tells us the most important job is "not to be governor." He then goes even further into this process of denial when he adds, "or first lady, in my case." This is a man deeply confused about his own sexuality. Like the time he introduced Senator Bill Frist in Nashville on May 27, 2004, and went on to add: "He married a Texas girl, I want you to know. Karyn is with us. A West Texas girl, just like me."

Rutherford: An instructive example. Well, the president may be confused in certain areas, but one topic he evidently understands is high finances. As he noted in May, 2000: "It's clearly a budget. It's got a lot of numbers in it." And in September of the same year: "More and more of our imports are coming from overseas." Clearly, those words indicate a profound grasp of economics as a whole. Yet it's when he talks about specific policies that his statements become more enigmatic. For instance, *The New York Times* quoted him in February, 2000 as saying: "I think we need not only to eliminate the tollbooth to the middle class, I think we should knock down the tollbooth." Any thoughts on this? Yes – Dr. Lao?

Lao: The Master is telling us to eliminate worldly possessions, and embrace the spiritual path. As the Tao reminds us: "If the fountains do not remain filled, they will be likely to dry up."

Tulley: I believe the president also intends a Biblical allusion here, to the time when Our Lord threw the moneylenders and tax-collectors out of the Temple.

Rutherford: Interesting comparison. Dr. Hoffmeier?

Hoffmeier: I see this as an unconscious reference to his wayward driving habits, during his college days. It's clear there's a lot of internal anger and resentment directed towards tollbooths here, perhaps combined with a suppressed memory of knocking one down on a late-night drive back to the dorm.

Rutherford: Various interpretations are possible, then. Turning next to the environment, George W. Bush remarked in reference to the Kyoto protocol: "We would not accept a treaty that would not have been ratified, nor a treaty that I thought made sense for the country." Any takers? Dr. Hoffmeier.

Hoffmeier: Once again, we see another symptom of the inferiority complex. Rather than face possible rejection by accepting a treaty that might not be ratified, he instead rejects it himself, even if the treaty would have made sense for the country. It's related to Groucho Marx's famous remark: "I wouldn't belong to any club that would have me as a member."

Rutherford: Do you agree, Dr. Lao? Was Bush right not to accept a treaty that would have made sense for the country?

Lao: As the Master revealed to us on August 8, 2003: "Sometimes pure politics enters into the rhetoric."

Rutherford: Point taken. Turning finally, then, to education, George W. Bush announced on January 11, 2000: "Rarely is the question asked: 'Is our children learning?'"

Lao: Perhaps he feels the question "Is our children learning?" is rarely asked precisely because people are so well educated.

Rutherford: So the observation is correct, then? The question *is* rarely asked?

Lao: The Master speaks wisely.

Tulley: Perhaps, too, he sees all children as one, under God; hence his use of the singular.

Hoffmeier: I see here a deep-seated fear about asking questions of any kind. This perhaps stems from his own schooldays, when he didn't want to appear foolish. And then he unconsciously provides exactly the kind of question he feared he might ask. So his use of the singular – "is" our children learning – refers here to his preoccupation with the ego and his fixation on his own educational insecurity.

Rutherford: Yet he seems to have gained some confidence in that area, does he not, when he proclaimed later the same year: "As governor of Texas, I have set high standards for our public schools, and I have met those standards"?

Hoffmeier: This shows us his therapy has proved successful. His misuse of the singular in an educational context has been all but eliminated, as we see from this quote of January 23, 2004:

"Then you wake up at the high school level and find out that the illiteracy level of our children are appalling." Although, as we might note, the association for Mr. Bush between "high school" and finding himself suddenly "waking up" remains strong.

Rutherford: And, of course, as he pointed out on July 10, 2001: "The great thing about America is you don't have to listen unless you want to." No doubt this observation has served him well, dating back to his early years. Well, I see we're almost out of time, so I'd like to ask each of you for one final quote that sums up the essence of George W. Bush for you personally. Reverend Tulley?

Tulley: I think one of my favorite quotes is when he told some visitors to the Oval Office on June 18, 2001: "The power that be – well, most of the power that be – sits right here." He's establishing his close personal relationship with the Almighty, yet he concedes that they each have a vital part to play in shaping the future of this great country.

Rutherford: Nice example. Dr. Lao?

Lao: On August 13, 2002, the Master revealed: "I promise you I will listen to what has been said here, even though I wasn't here." In this way, he shows us that all obstacles can be overcome. Just as insufficient votes can still win an election, or insufficient international support can still justify a foreign invasion, so insufficient physical presence creates no barrier to hearing the words of the people.

Rutherford: Very good. Dr. Hoffmeier?

Hoffmeier: One instructive moment, I think, came on Oct. 31, 2000, when he said: "Never again in the halls of Washington, D.C., do I want to have to make explanations that I can't explain." The point here, of course, is that he doesn't want to *have* to. He wants the option to remain open; indeed, he's exercised that option many times since becoming president. But, when it comes to making explanations he can't explain, he doesn't want to feel *compelled*. And I think, at some deep-seated level, the same holds true for all of us.

Rutherford: And there we must leave it. Thank you, all. Finally, as George W. Bush remarked in January, 2001, describing how he would feel upon assuming the presidency: "It'll be hard to articulate." I think we can safely conclude that truer words were never spoken.

5

ALIENS STOLE BUSH'S BRAIN
101 Reasons Why None Of This Is Bush's Fault

Art Lavinsky, Bureau of Internal Affairs, Washington, D.C.

I don't know about you, but I'm tired of all this Bush-bashing I've been hearing lately. Someone's got to stick up for George W. Bush. And it looks like that person is me.

Sure, these last few years have been rough on a lot of us. The president included. You think it's easy plunging our nation into the worst budget deficit in world history? Or trying to look concerned on TV about job outsourcing? Those things take their toll.

I want to make one thing clear from the beginning. This is not a president who makes excuses. Mind you, if ever a president had a series of legitimate excuses at his disposal, that president is George W. Bush.

Let me start with an item that, until recently, has been strictly classified by the CIA. Now that news of the incident has started to leak out to the media, our bureau feels it's important to set the record straight.

As many people have suspected for some time: Aliens stole Bush's brain. Now, think about that for a minute. How would *you* like to try running a country with nothing but empty space inside your head? It would be hard enough doing it for a single day; yet Bush has been doing it for years. And you don't hear *him* complain, do you? No, sir. He gets right on with his job. Just like you should be getting on with yours. Assuming it hasn't already been outsourced.

And if it has … well, believe me when I say that the president is very, very concerned.

Besides, as the president has been telling us all along, the economy is improving. All those jobs being outsourced today will soon be opening right back up again here at home. So those people aren't really jobless. They're just "between jobs."

But to get back to the president's brain. There's been a degree of controversy as to when the theft actually took place. For reasons of national security, I'm not authorized to reveal the exact date; nor can I reveal the method used by the aliens for the brain's removal. Fortunately, though, the after-effects have been minimal. Our enemies have analyzed video footage of George W. Bush taken at various times during his presidency, in the hope of gaining classified information related to the theft, and I'm pleased to report that so far they've made no progress. It's surprisingly hard to tell, even for a trained psychiatrist.

Which brings up another question: why would aliens want Bush's brain? It doesn't really have many uses. Even the president himself hardly used it during the years he had it. Perhaps, for the aliens, that was all part of the attraction. "Brain: Recreational use only. Single owner, non-intellectual, minimal frontal cortex overload. Like new. Make offer."

As it turned out, though, the incident resulted in a truly significant and far-reaching achievement. The president's brain ended up laying the foundation for a major interplanetary accord. I have here a copy of a previously classified communication from the planet Zargon, concerning the president's brain, which I will now read to you:

> Greetings, Earthlings!
> You'll be glad to know the Brain is a runaway hit on our planet. It has created its own sub-genre of family entertainment. Upon our return home, we took it immediately to one of our top cloning centers for

duplication and public distribution. We're in full production 28 hours a day, and we just can't keep them on the shelves. Everybody wants one! They're the hottest gift item of the year. Retail sales are up 17 percent this season, thanks largely to the Brain. Its thought-patterns provide a continuing source of mirth for the entire family, adults and children alike.

Our post-op observers on your planet have been monitoring the Brain's donor, and they have detected virtually no adverse effects since the Brain's removal. We doubt if most of your planet's inhabitants will even notice any change.

We can't thank you enough for the Brain. We were sorry to hear that your president is universally despised in all other countries on your planet, and in about 49 percent of your own country, as well. We would be glad to send clones of the Brain to these people, if you thought this would amuse them and help to change their minds. You may not have many allies left at home, but don't worry: if you can supply products of this caliber, you can always count on us for support.

Please tell the Brain's donor to have plenty of children. Genetic material like this is simply too priceless to waste!

Sincerely,

Your friends on the Zargon Planetary Entertainment Council

There. Who says the president doesn't know how to make alliances? Take that, Jacques Chirac! Personally, I think President Bush has done a remarkable job, especially considering he's been brainless for most of his term of office. You think it's easy? It's not! People just don't give the guy enough credit.

Besides, he's not really "brainless." He's just "between brains."

What's more, it hasn't slowed him down for a moment. A

complete absence of synaptic connections in the frontal lobes would take a heavy toll on the job performance of most presidents. But not George W. Bush. First of all, he's been in training for just such a situation all his life; and secondly, it has helped to take his mind off (quite literally!) the many, many other circumstances that might have brought down a lesser occupant of the Oval Office.

To begin with, he had to live down the Clinton economic legacy. As you may recall, Bill Clinton balanced the federal budget in just eight years, not only erasing a record budget deficit inherited from his predecessor, but even going on from there to create a record surplus. Well, that was just plain mean. His sole purpose in doing this was to make the Republicans look bad. What a show-off! Sure, *Clinton* could balance the budget. He was an economics major and a Rhodes Scholar, with an IQ way up in the triple digits. But he knew Bush couldn't do it.

Now, Bush may seem as dumb as a box of rocks, but he's not stupid. He wasn't about to get drawn into a sucker punch like that. So he followed the only remaining course of action open to him. He took all of Clinton's budget surplus, and spent the whole thing on tax giveaways for the richest people he could find. That took him back to zero. But then he realized Clinton didn't start at zero. Clinton started with a *deficit*. So then Bush had to go back to the Treasury and take out a whole lot more money, and spend it on even bigger tax cuts for the rich ... not to mention invading Afghanistan. That brought him right back down to where Clinton had started from. But then he realized that, if Clinton hadn't interfered, the budget deficit would now be far, far worse. So then he had to go back to the Treasury *again*, and take out a whole lot *more* money, and set about making all of those tax cuts permanent ... not to mention invading Iraq. So now he was finally down to the record deficit the country *would* have had if the Clinton Administration had never happened. That way, when he finally succeeds in balancing the budget again, he will have done it *all by himself*.

But, of course, we wouldn't be in this situation in the first place, would we, if the Democrats hadn't tried to hog the limelight? If they'd just shared the glory a little, and let *Bush* balance the budget, everything would have worked out fine. But no. Hog, hog, hog: that was the Democrats during the 1990s. That's why the Republican Congress fought Clinton all the way, during those eight long years of budget balancing. They could just see he was going to take all the budget-balancing credit for himself.

The nerve of the man!

So, as you can see, the deficit is really Clinton's fault. The point can't be stressed often enough.

But, of course, the economy isn't the only area where Bush has his excuses firmly nailed down. There's also the war in Iraq. In fact, as far as legitimate excuses go, that's probably his most impressive collection to date.

First of all, in terms of his handling of the war itself, let's get one major excuse right out on the table. Bush doesn't have a war record. That's right. Never seen active combat in his life. He has no idea how to go about it. Nor does Dick Cheney. Nor Karl Rove. None of them do. No clue what war's all about. None. *Nada.*

So is it really fair to blame these guys for every little miscalculation?

Not that Bush didn't try to get himself a war record, while he had the chance. Sure, he was handed that deferment into the National Guard, so he wouldn't get drafted and have to go to Vietnam. But he fought that deferment tooth and nail, right from the start. He was AWOL for months at a time, hoping the military would discipline him by shipping him off to 'Nam with his blue-collar buddies. But it was not to be. A blind eye here, a slap on the wrist there ... what's a guy to do? At least he tried.

So, after a frustrating experience like that, you can see why he didn't want John Kerry winning the election and showing him up on the war, just like Clinton did on the economy.

Of course, the president's repertoire of war excuses isn't limited to mere issues of strategy and bomb-dropping. There's also the important question of justification. And that's where President Bush showed his true colors as an excuse-maker *extraordinaire*.

Some people simply have a knack for finding an excuse other people may have overlooked. Fortunately for the world at large, President Bush happens to be one of those people. That's how he was able to inform the American voting public that Iraq had weapons of mass destruction.

It's true that these weapons of mass destruction were never found, even by international teams of weapons experts who scoured the country for months, acting on tips from the CIA, the Bush Administration, and other acknowledged sources. But that's what makes Bush's talent so remarkable. He can put his finger squarely on the truth, even in the absence of corroborating evidence. That's what makes him a great president.

Admittedly, the Iraqis maintained all along that they'd complied with international agreement by dismantling all of their weapons of mass destruction, as well as their capabilities for manufacturing them. Luckily, President Bush – a man who knows a lie when he hears one – was able to see right through that claim and declare war anyway, thereby cleverly preventing a military debacle in the Middle East, and also safeguarding America's world reputation.

Of course, Iraq did have weapons of mass destruction in the past. They've admitted that already. After all, Saddam Hussein used chemical weapons during the 1980s, in his war against Iran (which is a totally separate country from Iraq, despite the similar names, as President Bush is now fully aware). In other words, we've known about the Iraq weapons situation for some time. Which means President Bush wouldn't have needed to invade Iraq at all, if Clinton had just taken a little responsibility, and acted earlier. So, as you can see, the fact that we're currently involved in a war with Iraq is technically Clinton's fault, as well.

But all of the excuses I've cited so far have the same minor flaw. They pertain only to one specific circumstance (the economy, the war, etc.) When it comes to excuses, President George W. Bush is a professional. He wanted an excuse he could count on, day and night: a one-size-fits-all panacea he could trot out any time he needed it, without having to stop and think.

Naturally, with his talent, it didn't take him long to come up with a work of art in that regard. A true masterpiece. A Rembrandt among excuses. All bound up in six little words:

God told me to do it.

There. If that isn't the grand-daddy of all presidential excuses, I don't know what is. It works in literally any and all situations. "God told me to do it." *Voilà*. End of discussion. Works every time.

And people say Bush isn't a genius!

In fact, that very point, in itself, brings up one of the president's most legitimate excuses of all: the fact that people are continually making fun of him for appearing slow on the uptake.

Well, think about it. When aliens have stolen your brain, you're bound to get caught on camera looking a little vacant now and again.

It certainly didn't help him in the presidential debates. I mean, *you* try debating with one of those prompter things bulging under your suit jacket. All the time trying to think of what to say, while someone else is yakking in your ear. No wonder he came across looking like an imbecile.

And it wasn't just the debates. This has been an ongoing problem for years. Admittedly, the "Bush look" has its unique features. In some newspaper cartoons, for instance, George W. Bush has even been compared – unfairly, I need hardly say – to a chimpanzee.

This is unfair partly because, like every other member of the human race (including you and me), George W. Bush shares approximately 99 percent of his DNA with chimpanzees. Statistically, of course, that percentage may be slightly higher or lower in certain cases. You decide.

In any case, George W. Bush doesn't look anything like a chimpanzee. He looks more like a ... well, more like ... well, let's see. More of a ... well ...

Well, moving on, anyway.

I regret I don't have time to present all 101 of the president's excuses today. Besides, as some of you may have already guessed, the actual total is not 101. For reasons of national security, I'm not authorized to reveal the precise number. But I'd like to end with one more top-flight excuse from the George W. Bush legacy. I think you'll agree this final excuse I'm going to present is particularly compelling in terms of condoning any possible misjudgments or miscalculations President Bush may or may not have made during his years in office.

Quite simply: He's always getting blamed for everything by the liberal media.

That's right. The liberal gutter press simply can't wait to drag our president through the mud over every allegation of greed or callous indifference – no matter how minor. You can imagine how that must make his job ten times harder! Those reporters ought to acknowledge the president's excuses a little more openly, before rushing to judgment over every election fraud scandal or Geneva Convention infringement.

I mean, let's be serious here. Would George W. Bush, that pinnacle of American morality, have faltered even for a moment on his handling of the economy, the environment, civil rights, the war in Iraq, the "peace" in Iraq, the prison camps in Iraq, America's global reputation, etc., if he'd had a different set of resources available to him? Suppose he'd had, at his disposal, a full complement of brain cells, or some sense of human compassion, or the ability to spot an economic disaster in the making? Should we really hold our president accountable for crises so clearly outside his control? Or should we just give him the benefit of the doubt, and attribute his occasional misstep to a series of unfortunate but unavoidable circumstances?

I say, give him the benefit of the doubt.

He's only human, after all.

Well, at least 99 percent.

6

SPRINGTIME FOR BÜSHLER
A Washington Impostor Reinvents The Big Lie Principle

Emily Robertson-Santiago, American Civil Liberties Union

George W. Bush was never actually President of the United States. I'm not talking about Florida 2000, or Ohio 2004. Sure, there was all that, too. But I'm talking about a far more devious, more closely guarded secret: the fact that, for the entire duration of the so-called "George W. Bush" presidency, the White House has been occupied by an impostor.

But let's not rush in. Let's first consider the integrity of the *real* George W. Bush.

❦ A Yale graduate. Did you know that such was George W.'s academic standing at Yale, that he even participated in a voluntary program to test the effects of substance abuse on the human brain? That's the kind of man we're talking about here.

❦ An honorably discharged veteran of the Vietnam Era. So vital, in fact, was George W.'s contribution to national security that he was granted a special deferment from his military duties so he could participate in a Republican political campaign.

And the list goes on. I mean, is this guy Mr. Respectable, or what? Let's face it, George W. Bush is a Prince among Men. A veritable Bastion of Society.

How, then, could anyone seriously claim that this same George W. Bush would ignore urgent CIA memos with titles like "Bin Laden Determined to Strike in U.S."?

Then factor in the so-called "Bush" Administration's handling of the war in Iraq, the economy, the environment, America's world reputation ... and a disturbing pattern begins to emerge.

Can we seriously attribute each and every one of these catastrophes to George W. Bush?

It just doesn't seem likely, does it? Which leaves us with only one viable alternative: an impostor in the White House.

I admit, that leaves a few lingering questions. If he's not George W. Bush, who the heck *is* this guy? How could something like this ever happen? And, even if it did happen, how come the real George W. Bush didn't speak up years ago?

To answer these questions, we must first consider the Republican Party of 2000. They desperately wanted to win back the White House, and restore the glory days of trickle-down economics (*translation*: give a lot of your money to rich people). But, to succeed, they needed two things from their candidate.

First, they needed a man of honor: a caring, compassionate conservative who would pledge to safeguard social security, build on the Clinton budget surplus, provide jobs for our nation's families, protect civil rights, and lift America's global reputation to new and dizzying heights. In short, who better than George W. Bush, aforementioned Bastion of Society and Prince among Men?

Second, they needed a candidate who would willingly embrace their nefarious schemes for economic plunder, social divisiveness, and unlawful military expansionism.

Ah. There lay the rub.

A man of the Ivy-League intellect and steadfast moral character of George W. would never endorse such a plan. On the other hand, any candidate who *would* endorse such a plan would be unelectable.

What the Republicans needed was a cunning combination of the two. The proud name and unblemished reputation of George W. Bush on the ticket, followed by the old switcheroo.

Exit George W., with a loyal Republican promise of silence.
Enter Adolf Büshler.
Büshler, you see, was the perfect choice. First of all, he turned

out (incredibly conveniently) to be a lineal descendant of Adolf Hitler, so ideas like economic plunder, social divisiveness and unlawful military expansionism simply came naturally. They didn't even have to be explained.

Even more conveniently, this Büshler bore an uncanny physical resemblance to the real George W. Bush.

It must have been just too tempting to resist. A touch of plastic surgery here, a trace of makeup there, and Büshler would be good to go. You can imagine how those Republican back-room schemers would have begun tapping their fingernails and hatching their Bush-impersonation plots without so much as a backward glance.

As to why the real George W. didn't speak up? Well, think about it. George W. Bush is a loyal Republican, a party man, a true-blue America-first kind of guy, who probably thought to himself: *Heck, if the Republican Party thinks this would be good for America, then I'd prefer to keep quiet and let them sully my good name in the interests of corporate profit, rather than speak out and stand in the way of the greater good.* Selfless? Yes. But that's George. That's George W., my friends. Loyal, dedicated ... a Republican's Republican, through and through.

But back to Büshler.

All politicians lie now and then. For most, lying is a mere convenience. But the organized web of lies put out by the Büshler Administration has created an ominous escalation of scale.

This isn't just: "I didn't have an affair with an intern."

It isn't even just: "I am not a crook."

No. This is a systematic effort to deceive and defraud the American public for personal and political gain.

To borrow John Kerry's phrase: "A Weapon of Mass Deception."

Of course, this kind of deliberate, widespread misinformation – the "Big Lie" Principle – is generally associated with totalitarian regimes. As Lenin put it: "A lie told often enough becomes truth." And then there's the man who practically invented the Big Lie

Principle: Adolf Hitler.

The Big Lie Principle is very simple. You don't tell small lies. You don't tell occasional lies. You don't tell selective lies. You tell monstrous, calculated lies about every single aspect of your regime. And then you repeat them, over and over and over.

"My tax cuts will benefit all Americans."

"No Child Left Behind."

"Operation Iraqi Freedom."

"I'm a uniter, not a divider."

Pretty soon, these lies start to become familiar. People know they've heard them somewhere before. And they start to believe them.

But I know what you're thinking. *Büshler may be a terrible president – arguably the worst in U.S. history – but he's no Adolf Hitler. I mean ... IS he?*

Well, you're probably right. Still, just to be on the safe side, we should probably take a closer look. We'll compare the Ten Biggest Lies of Büshler and Hitler, and draw our own conclusions.

Big Lie #1: Establish a credible outside threat to national security.

Remember, the idea here is to instill fear into the public.

Fear is a powerful motivator. It molds the public to your will. It makes people look to their leaders in times of crisis. It wins elections.

Let's say that last sentence again.

It wins elections.

Oh, sure, you still might have to do a little vote-rigging in key battleground states like Ohio, just to ensure victory. But, by and large, fear helps keep you in power.

Especially if you keep repeating, over and over, the importance of not changing leaders in the middle of a crisis.

Never mind that you're the leader who got us into this crisis in the first place.

You don't mention *that*. Good God, no!

Keep the public fearful and obedient at all times. That's the ticket.

Clearly, then, it has to be a *credible* threat to national security. Something nice and convincing.

Hitler came up with a great one. Russia. That looming superpower to the East, full of Communists, just the other side of Poland. ("Hmm ... better take a memo, Eva: 'Annex Poland sometime soon.'")

But Russia wouldn't quite do for Büshler. He needed something slightly more ... well, shall we say, *au courant*.

Something real. Something nasty. Something he could point to.

You can just imagine his mind grinding into gear:

"Let's see, now. Maybe if I ignore those CIA warnings about Osama bin Laden, I can use the extra time to come up with an idea ..."

Big Lie #2: Identify foreign countries you want to invade, and then claim you need to invade them as a matter of "national security."

Let's face it. If you're any kind of self-respecting dictator, you probably have a whole list of countries you're simply itching to invade. (Oh, come on. You can think of at least *one*.)

Unfortunately, you can't just barge ahead. The first rule of any major international military offensive is that you need what is known, in the biz, as "justification."

A snag, yes. But not insurmountable. Not if you've laid your groundwork properly.

You see, that's where Big Lie #1 comes in so handy. Establish a credible outside threat to national security, and bingo! Justification City.

Now, don't make the rookie-dictator mistake of confusing "justification" with "your real reason for wanting to invade." Those are two very different things.

"Justification" is what you tell the public.

"Your real reason" is another matter.

To clarify, let's look at a couple of actual historical invasions:

1939: Hitler invades Poland.

Justification: "The Polish threat is too immediate to ignore. It's a matter of national security."

Real reasons: First, Hitler needed land for food, and Poland provided the perfect breadbasket. Second, he could start spreading the doctrine of Nazism beyond Germany's borders. Third, he could "test the waters," and gauge international reaction. If he got away with Poland, then: Hello, Belgium.

2003: Büshler invades Iraq.

Justification: "The terrorist threat is too immediate to ignore. Iraq has weapons of mass destruction. It's a matter of national security."

Real reasons: First, as an oil tycoon, Büshler naturally wanted to invade an oil-rich nation. Second, he and his pals could award "good ol' buddy" companies like Halliburton billions of public dollars for post-war reconstruction. Third, he cleverly disguised his *real* invasion target by invading Afghanistan *first*. He got away with Afghanistan, so: Hello, Iraq.

Don't forget, too, that wars are amazingly popular when it comes to re-election campaigns. Never mind the casualties. Never mind the fact that those casualties are your fault. Just keep up the war rhetoric. It really works!

And as an added bonus: if you're accused of election fraud (and, face it, you're bound to get caught *somewhere*), you can always step up a major bombing raid just to distract public attention.

Timing is everything.

Big Lie #3: Promote a climate of extreme patriotic fervor across the country.

Hitler called it "nationalism." Büshler calls it "patriotism." Either way, it's the same idea. You appeal to the basest tribal instincts of the public, goading your followers into an animalistic display of "patriotic" frenzy:

"Us against Them."

"Christian against Muslim."

"Evangelical against Gay."

Note how conveniently this also ties into every dictator's dream of social divisiveness and public persecution. (We'll come to that in Big Lie #4).

Meanwhile, so far, so good. You've got the party faithful baying for blood. Now comes the important part. In the minds of the public, you connect this idea of "patriotism" with the idea of unswerving, knee-jerk support for you and your regime. Anyone who is not with you is against you, and therefore unpatriotic.

That's the point. Against you, *and therefore unpatriotic*.

Keep repeating that until people believe it.

And one more thing. For best results, you also need to claim that you're uniting the country.

Hitler had it easy here. In Hitler's day, Germany was a young country, founded just a couple of generations earlier. There were lots of preexisting divisions. They were still torn by their recent defeat in World War I. This was a country crying out for unification. All Hitler had to do was preach the nationalist doctrine, tap into a long-standing undercurrent of anti-Semitism, and find a way to go to war. After that, he was home free.

Büshler cleverly avoided copyright infringement by preaching a doctrine of patriotism, tapping into a long-standing undercurrent of homophobia, and finding a way to go to war. (Well, OK, that last one's pretty much in the public domain.)

But Büshler faced one problem Hitler didn't, in terms of promising to unite the country. The problem was, quite simply: America was united already. So Büshler first had to *divide* the country on ideological grounds, right down the middle, in order for his promise of uniting the country to carry some weight.

Which is where barefaced lies like "I'm a uniter, not a divider" come in so very handy.

For sheer audacity, that's quite a claim, isn't it?

Note that there's no need to explain exactly *how* you are uniting the country. The reason for this is simple. The more you divide the country first, the more people will want the country to be united, and will flock to a leader who promises to unite it.

See how it works?

Same thing with the war. We wouldn't want to change leaders in the middle of a crisis, would we? Better stick with the walking catastrophe who got us into this mess in the first place.

Same with the economy. Büshler inherited our nation's greatest-ever budget surplus from Clinton, and wasted no time in transforming it into a Social-Security-raiding, migraine-inducing, all-time-record deficit. Clearly, this stud *hombre* knows what he's doing! Why trust our floundering economy to anyone else?

Excuse me ... but has the entire planet gone insane?

Big Lie #4: Identify unpopular minority groups, and gain political leverage by persecuting them "for the good of society."

In 1935, Hitler pushed through the so-called "Nuremberg Laws," amending Germany's equivalent of a Constitution by depriving Jews of most of their civil rights. Notable among these amendments was a mandated restriction on exactly who Jews could or could not marry.

Anyone notice a familiar trend?

Big Lie #5: Centralize your secret security forces as a ploy to erode human rights.

Consider the following. In 1936, Hitler took another giant step towards his persecution and control of minorities. He consolidated the SS (his black-uniformed elite militia) and the Gestapo (his secret police) into one unified agency, and appointed his trusted friend, Heinrich Himmler, to run it. He didn't actually come up with a phrase like "Security Czar," but you get the idea.

Now, the Gestapo weren't exactly "secret." Their *activities* were secret, yes. But the Gestapo themselves were well-known throughout Germany.

What the German people *didn't* know, however, was that the new, unified agency had an ultra-secret higher echelon, called the SD. It was the SD, under Himmler, that perpetrated the real atrocities of the Nazi regime.

Luckily, that kind of thing could never happen here in the United States of America, because we have – *drum roll, please* – a Constitution!

Of course, during Büshler's first term of office, we also had an Attorney General who considered the Constitution a pesky interference with his duties, and could hardly wait to try out the Big Scissors on it.

Well, not all of it, of course. Nothing wrong with the Right to Bear Arms. The more rounds per minute, the merrier.

But take the First Amendment, for instance.

Freedom of Speech? What's up with *that*? We're trying to run a country here!

Freedom of Religion? You've *got* to be kidding. Right?

And the list goes on! Freedom of *Assembly*??

OK. Let's hold it right there.

Let me tell you a little story about Freedom of Assembly.

In 2003, when Büshler was launching his oil-invasion of Iraq – sorry, I mean "Operation Iraqi Freedom" – peaceful demonstrations sprang up in cities all over the country to protest the war. Most of these lasted two or three hours, but the one in Portland, Oregon lasted well after dark. People watched their TVs with pride, glad that our Constitutional First Amendment rights were still alive and well in the World's Greatest Democracy. Because it was, as I say, a peaceful protest. No clashes with police. Nothing like that.

And then came the word from the Büshlerites. Because America was now in a state of war, the special provisions of the Patriot Act allowed them to raise the penalty for "civil disobedience" – even a peaceful demonstration like this one – to life imprisonment.

Uh-huh. That's literally what they said.

It was even darkly hinted that the death penalty might be invoked.

Ah, yes. The good old Patriot Act. Apparently, all Büshler has to do under the Patriot Act, to keep those "special provisions" going, is to ensure that the U.S. is perpetually in a "state of war."

That shouldn't be hard. There are plenty of other countries we can invade, even if the last man standing in Iraq goes down. And, these days, we don't even need the approval of the United Nations. All we need is a pin, an atlas, and a blindfold.

Meanwhile, let's hurry up and get that Security Czar appointed! Don't you just feel safe in Büshler's America?

Big Lie #6: Proclaim you are improving the education system, while working to undermine it.

An uneducated public is a gullible public.

An ignorant, misinformed public will believe every lie you utter, and will turn out for you at the voting booths, like obedient little sheep.

Baaa-a-a-aa.

Büüü-ü-ü-üshler.

So, how to keep them ignorant and misinformed?

The secret is to get 'em while they're young.

Here's your opening salvo. First, you introduce a lot of red-tape federal legislation regarding mandatory grade-level testing and inclusion of students with disabilities. Then you dress it up in a nice, feel-good package. Give it a catchy name. Something like … No Child Left Behind. You garner bipartisan support for it in the U.S. Senate. Get yourself photographed shaking hands over it with Senator Edward Kennedy.

Then you pull the rug. Hard. You drastically underfund it, leaving financially strapped school districts scrambling so fast to comply with the new legislation that they fall even further behind in their actual job of educating our nation's children.

And then you play your trump card. With the school system brought to its knees, you move in to indoctrinate. Early and often.

School prayer. The Pledge of Allegiance. No teaching of

evolution. Step by step, you chip away at the twin evils of Scholarship and Religious Freedom.

Incidentally, does anyone else find it ironic that the same president who wants to ban the teaching of evolution in our public schools also happens to be a walking poster-child for the idea that humans are descended from apes?

Early and often. That's the way to indoctrinate.

No one understood that better than Hitler. Under Hitler, what you could and couldn't teach was strictly regulated by the Gestapo. Children were required to use the standard greeting of *Heil Hitler!*, even when addressing one another.

No Child Left Behind in 1930s Germany, I can assure you. All equally indoctrinated, under the law.

Big Lie #7: Take other people's money, and distribute it to yourself and your supporters.

Let's be frank. That's really what it's all about, isn't it?

Big Lie #8: Steal power any way you can, and legitimize your actions later.

In the German national election of 1933, Hitler failed to win a majority, so he had to resort to legal chicanery. He convinced the Parliament that the Communist threat was real, and pushed through a vote to have all of the Communist members immediately expelled from Government. That gave him a narrow majority. Then, despite having failed to win the popular vote, he refused to compromise on any policies, and railroaded a law through Parliament to consolidate his own powers.

In the U.S. national election of 2000, Büshler failed to win a majority, so he had to resort to legal chicanery. He convinced the Supreme Court to ignore claims of voter fraud in Florida, and award all of the state's electoral votes to his campaign. That gave him a narrow majority. Then, despite having failed to win the popular vote, he refused to compromise on any policies, and railroaded the Patriot Act through Congress to consolidate his own powers.

Hitler called it a "legal revolution."

Büshler called it a "free and fair election."

And, talking of the Patriot Act ... have you ever actually read it?

If you haven't, you're in good company. Very good company. Almost the entire known universe, in fact. Including – at least at the time the Act was passed – most of the Congress who voted it into law.

For one thing, the Patriot Act has 159 sections of detailed, cross-referenced information. It's also intentionally evasive. Its authors have gone out of their way to ensure that anyone reading it won't understand the finer points, unless they have a stack of weighty legal reference material right at their elbows. All of which takes time to wade through.

The Büshler Administration knew that perfectly well. So they made sure time was one thing Congress didn't have, when voting on the Patriot Act.

Here's what happened, back in October, 2001:

Attorney General John Ashcroft managed to slither his version of the Patriot Act directly to the Senate floor. No discussion. No debate. No hearings. As you can imagine, many Senators complained about being railroaded into voting on a bill of such far-reaching consequence, without being given much of a chance to read it. Let alone dig up the stack of weighty legal reference material they would need to analyze it in any meaningful way.

Such analysis, of course, was exactly what the Büshler Administration wanted to avoid. Remember, this was just a few weeks after the terrorist attacks of September 11. What better time to exploit a national climate of fear and uncertainty? ("Quick! Hurry! Pass the Patriot Act, before they strike again! No time to read it, Senator! If you vote against it, the next attack will be *your fault!*")

And remember the anthrax letters? All of that was happening around the same time.

Remember who *got* the anthrax letters?

Probably all those high-ranking Republicans who were pushing through this anti-terrorist legislation. They'd be prime terrorist targets. Right?

Wrong.

Senator Tom Daschle, the ranking Democrat in the Senate, staunch civil rights watchdog and defender of the U.S. Constitution. And the major national media: the kind of people who might snoop around and investigate the Patriot act a little too closely. Got to keep *them* busy.

("So, hurry up, Senators! And remember, there's an anthrax letter in the mail for every bad boy or girl who votes against the Patriot Act!")

Over in the House of Representatives, things were proceeding at a more controlled pace. Hearings were held. A compromise bill was worked out. But, of course, the hard-line Republican House leadership only allowed that little charade to go so far. They abruptly jettisoned the compromise bill, and replaced it with the Ashcroft-Senate version. No discussion. No debate. No hearings. As with the Senate, members of the House were given virtually no time to read the "revised" bill before a vote was called.

Mission Accomplished.

Except ... how did the Patriot Act's authors manage to cobble together all of those 159 sections so quickly?

The answer is simple. *Much of it was written in advance.* That's right. Prior to 9/11. And then the Büshler Administration conveniently railroaded the Patriot Act into law during a climate of national hysteria.

You see, much of the Patriot Act isn't really about terrorism at all. Some of it is. Quite a lot of it is, actually. But many of those 159 sections are more concerned with granting the President extraordinary powers. Or allowing secret surveillance of U.S. citizens without due process or reasonable cause. Or reducing the power of the courts to hear grievances about government actions.

In fact, many of the clauses that found their way into the Patriot Act had already been voted down by Congress, prior to 9/11.

But not any more. What a lucky break for Büshler.

Big Lie #9: Claim that God is on your side.
The scary thing here isn't that Büshler spends time talking to God.

No. The scary thing is that God spends time talking to Büshler.

Big Lie #10: Stick to your lies, even when facts indicate the exact opposite.
Considering a rewarding career in the dictatorship business? Then heed this advice:

Never, *EVER* publicly admit you were wrong, or change your mind about anything.

You think Hitler admitted he was wrong? Quite the reverse. Back him into a corner, and he lashed out all the harder.

In 1934, when several members of his Nazi inner circle, including his close friend Ernst Röhm, accused him of moving too fast with his extremist policies, he simply had them murdered. He wasn't about to take that kind of sass from *anybody*.

As for changing his mind ... well, who knows what he thought in private? But he stayed the course, as any true dictator should.

Same thing with Büshler.

You don't see Büshler, on national TV, wringing his hands over the war, accepting blame for the casualties, lamenting the destruction of other people's property. Of course not. He *calculated* those things, in advance. All he cares about is the votes. Don't count on him conceding that his tax cuts for the rich sent our economy into a nosedive. Or losing sleep over those multibillion-dollar giveaways to Dick Cheney's hand-in-glove company, Halliburton. Or apologizing for his Bible-thumping exhortation to use the United States Constitution as a forum for bigotry and hate. Nope. All he cares about is the good old Electoral College.

Admitting any mistake, no matter how small, might cost him an election.

Of course, he takes plenty of additional precautions where elections are concerned. No worries there. ("Thanks, Republican Ohio vote-counters!")

Besides, why *should* Büshler admit he was wrong? On every one of those issues, he knew he was wrong *going in*. Why bother to admit it after the fact?

Amazingly enough, Büshler *did* admit – at the Republican National Convention, of all places – that we couldn't win the war on terror. Look how quickly he retracted that! His aides probably pulled him aside and told him, "Hey Adolf, you just can't say things like that! Not and get re-elected! The election's only ten weeks away! What were you thinking?"

Yeah. What *was* he thinking?

But then, most of us wonder that about Büshler on a regular basis. So nothing new there.

Of course, it wasn't exactly a "retraction," was it? Not from Büshler. It was a "clarification." He "clarified" that what he *really* meant was that we *could* win the war on terror, after all. He went on to clarify that this was the view he'd held all along, so it wasn't (technically) a flip-flop, since … well, since it was the view he'd held all along, and since … um … well, since he'd now clarified that this was what he'd really meant to say anyway. If you get the gist.

Believe me, a distraught nation was reassured to hear *those* words of comfort!

To sum up the Büshler philosophy:
1. When in doubt, lie.
2. When not in doubt, lie.
3. When caught in a lie, lie about lying.
4. Always accuse your opponents of lying, to create a diversion.
5. Above all, stick to your lies at all times.

So, in closing, let's revisit some of the Büshler Administration's greatest hits:

"Iraq Had Weapons Of Mass Destruction."
"No Child Left Behind."
"I'm A Uniter, Not A Divider."
"Mission Accomplished."
And, of course, the #1 blockbuster:
"Since Becoming Vice President, I've Had No Financial Interest In Halliburton Of Any Kind."

Ah. Those timeless classics. Somehow, they just never grow old.

See? It's easy and fun to run a totalitarian regime! You get to plunder the Treasury, declare war all around the globe, and persecute any minorities you feel like!

Life just couldn't get any better, could it?

As Büshler himself might say, if he suddenly found himself under the influence of a truth serum that forced him to stop lying for a few minutes, "My fellow Americans: There's a joy that comes from depriving people of their civil liberties, and I propose to indulge that joy to the fullest extent allowable by law. If necessary, I'll change the Constitution, to make that extent even fuller. Thank you, and good night."

7

THANK GOD THINGS ARE FINALLY LOOKING UP
Why George W. Bush Was Exactly What America Needed

William L. Thayer IV, President and CEO, Texas Armaments

There's never been a president quite like George W. Bush. And I mean that in a good way. Finally, we have a president who runs this country like a business.

Take the economy, for instance. Look at the state of affairs when George W. Bush took office. Sure, Clinton had built up a record surplus. But, from a business perspective, there's no long-term benefit to storing up capital. You need to make your money work for you, by investing in the most profitable assets available.

In America's case, those assets are the rich. That's why giving rich people a tax break was so important. Think about the return on your investment. Who's going to bring you in more revenue over the long term? Some Joe Schmo, trying to hang on to a part-time job at Wal-Mart? How much is *he* ever going to put back into the system? Or some wealthy capitalist entrepreneur? *There's* where you want to put your money. That was the logic behind the Bush decision to take all of our budget surplus – our "investment capital," if you will – and invest it in tax breaks for those with enough earning power to do something productive for America in return. Give money to people like that, and they can provide jobs for dozens of Joe Schmos. Hundreds, perhaps. Or thousands. Even as far away as India.

And that's another thing. People – and when I say "people"

here, I mean liberals – are always harping on about Bush's blue-sky policy on job outsourcing. They don't seem to realize it makes perfect business sense. American companies can hire foreign workers more cheaply, so profits rise, which benefits our entire economy.

And that's not all. Outsourcing also cools down the job market here at home, helping to bring domestic salaries more in line with those overseas. That way, when companies do hire American workers, they can hire more people and increase corporate profits at the same time. It's a win-win situation all around. The workers certainly aren't hurting from the deal. It's a lot better than collecting unemployment benefits which are about to run out – and, in some cases, already have. We may not be hiring them back at the salary they earned before getting laid off, but once they adjust, and learn to cut a few corners, they'll hardly know the difference. It's only a few thousand a year per employee, spread out over a large number of households. But look at the reward for the CEO who created those jobs in the first place. A million or two in profit-sharing bonuses can really make a difference, when you've got yachts and private planes and mansion payments to think about. Believe me, those things add up. We rich folk have expenses, just like everyone else. Beluga caviar doesn't come cheap – and the cat won't eat anything else, now that the kids have been spoiling her. Those little rascals.

And then there are hidden expenses most people don't even think about. Take the elder President Bush, for instance. He not only had to pay for his son's tuition at Yale – and that's a pretty penny – but he also made a substantial "donation" just to make comfortably sure his son could be admitted despite his GPA … and, for that matter, eventually graduate. So expenses come up, even for the rich. In fact, the deeper your pockets, the more they know they can get out of you. All we're asking America's workers to do is tighten their belts a little in these economic times, so the money can go to those few people who truly appreciate its value. It's not all that different from a state lottery system, really …

except that in this case the winners are predetermined.

Another liberal whine I hear a lot these days is about so-called "unaffordable" health care. Well, it's perfectly affordable if you set aside the money for it. *I* can afford it just fine. It's a question of learning how to budget. Besides, why should companies be expected to pay for employees' health care? That just cuts into the profit margins that keep America strong. It seems positively unpatriotic to ask corporations to fritter away money on luxuries like employee health benefits. If someone gets sick, you just hire someone else to take their place. Plenty of other people need those jobs. You're really doing the new person a favor.

Furthermore, you can't expect insurance companies to lower their premiums just to accommodate people's budgets. They've got their own profit margins to think about. I'm glad to see George W. Bush understands that. Same thing with the pharmaceutical companies. Why should they lower their drug prices fifty, sixty, seventy percent, just because that's what people pay for those drugs in Canada? Luckily, so long as the Republicans stay in power, those companies won't have to concede a penny. Just keep Hillary out of there, that's all I ask. People seem to view the drug industry as some kind of charity, providing medicines for people in need at affordable prices, with no thought whatever for corporate profits. And then they get all bent out of shape when some new drug turns out to have a harmful side effect, in spite of the manufacturer's best efforts. Sometimes I just shake my head in wonder, that people could be so naïve. Every day I'm thankful I work for an armaments company, where our products are *intended* to kill people. That way, there's no room for misunderstanding.

Now, at this point some of you Democrats may be thinking: How come we can't just have a *national* health care system, run by the government? Well, thank God we have George W. Bush to put a stop to *that* idea, too. Think about the cost to the taxpayers. Sure, we're the richest nation in the world. But one reason we're so rich is that we don't waste money on expendable people like the sick and the elderly. Honestly, if we didn't have Republicans to keep us on the right track, I swear this entire country would fall apart financially at the seams.

Of course, the main gripe we hear about these days is the war in Iraq. But, here again, you have to keep in mind that this war is a business venture. It's not about the casualties, or the so-called "cowboy" diplomacy. George Bush is simply looking out for America's corporate interests. And he's done it extremely well. The war may be costing the taxpayers a couple of billion a week, but frankly, Texas Armaments has come out of it very nicely. And we're not alone. Other companies, like Halliburton, would certainly agree with me here. The Iraq war and its related reconstruction costs have put a lot of money in the right corporate pockets, and will continue to do so for many years to come, even after George W. Bush is no longer president. Now, that's what I call an economic legacy.

Then there's the environment. How can people expect corporate America to do its job, when we're continually hamstrung by outmoded environmental regulations? Every dollar we throw at the environment could be much better spent creating new jobs. (In terms of financial planning, of course, we wouldn't actually invest in those new jobs right away. First, we'd need to grow our profit margin, and build investor confidence. This would then provide the capital to attract and retain effective top-level corporate management. Finally, thanks to trickle-down economics, we could expect to see job growth over the long term.) So, yes, it really is all about jobs. And that's why George W. Bush made it a priority, as soon as he took office, to throw out the environmental regulations that prevent corporate America from doing an effective, profitable business.

Same problem with the Kyoto Protocol. Think of the needless corporate expense of reducing air pollution, when our air is quite clean enough as it is. Besides, the United States has 5 percent of the world's population, and generates 35 percent of the greenhouse gases, so it's pretty obvious what kind of "message" the international community was trying to send. *We* were expected to bear the brunt of the cleanup costs! That's right: the Kyoto Protocol is one more example of rabid international anti-Americanism. Naturally, President George W. Bush gave *that* idea the brush-off it deserved. Heck, we're too busy fighting a war right now! Two, if you count Afghanistan. Well, soon to be three, of course, if you count Iran. And there's always North Korea, waiting in the wings. I mean, they really *do* have weapons of mass destruction. So does France, for that matter.

It's true that virtually every other industrialized country in the world has signed the Kyoto Protocol, and is actively investing resources to reduce pollution and lower the threat of global warming from greenhouse gases. But it won't cost America a dime ... and we still get to reap the benefits. To those other countries, I have only one thing to say: "Suckers!" Why give till you have to? It's the same with employee benefits. Keep 'em to a minimum, that's what I say. No company ever got rich by giving away the store.

One final liberal complaint I want to address tonight is the idea that George W. Bush doesn't make all of his own decisions. Well, of course he doesn't! How could one person be an expert on every aspect of U.S. policy? George Bush's main job, as president, is to delegate. In fact, he's even taken it one step further. He actually delegates most of the delegating, as well.

Now, much has been made of Karl Rove's involvement behind the scenes in the Oval Office. People talk as if he's some kind of master-puppeteer, pulling all the strings, while George W. Bush dances to the tune. I can assure you, that isn't the case at all. There are plenty of other people in Washington performing much the same function as Karl. Obviously, it would be ludicrous to have all that power concentrated in the hands of one man. Besides, there are large numbers of campaign donors and corporate lobbyists, all demanding a return on their election investment. Karl simply couldn't keep track of them all. He has to delegate, too.

Perhaps it would help to clarify Bush's role if I explained it in terms of the corporate environment. Take me, for example. I'm the president and CEO of Texas Armaments. But do you think I know about weapons manufacturing? I'm just the head honcho. My job is to increase corporate profits and attract major investors. Then those investors, in turn, tell me what to do, and pay me accordingly. It's their money, after all. Same story over at Enron. And WorldCom. All good, solid companies, headed up by the kind of people who know the Bushes personally.

I realize Enron and WorldCom have been in the news regarding allegations of financial misconduct. But really, all they did was borrow a little petty cash I'm sure they fully intended to return. You know how it is. Expenses come up, and suddenly you need a million or two overnight. It's not easy, living the rich lifestyle. I mean, we've got nannies and babysitters and governesses and tutors to think of. Next, you'll be asking us to raise our own children! And then we've got all those time-shares in Barbados and Acapulco and the French Riviera to cash in, before our window of availability closes for the year. We're rich. It's what we do.

So, next time you read about top executive salaries, or tax breaks for the rich, just remember: we have to make our budgets stretch, just the same as you do. So, spare us a thought, and don't forget to vote Republican. Thank you very much.

8

GEORGE W. BUSH: MYTH, MONSTER, OR MARIONETTE?
CONCLUDING REMARKS BY THE SYMPOSIUM CHAIR

Marian Rutherford, Ph.D., Professor of Philosophy, U.C. Berkeley

As we conclude today's George W. Bush Symposium, I invite you to look back and reflect upon the variety and wealth of new data we've heard presented here. As someone who has spent the past few years researching the nature and meaning – indeed, the very existence – of George W. Bush, I can tell you I was thrilled to take part in this remarkable voyage of discovery and exploration.

By all accounts, the empirical evidence that George W. Bush may truly exist is gathering momentum. Parallels have been noted with the last observed "Bush" presidency, which occurred during the late 1980s and early 1990s. Uncontrolled budget deficits, a war against Iraq, large-scale Pentagon contracts for Halliburton … these are all historical indicators of a George Bush in the White House.

As persuasive as this evidence may appear, however, I would urge caution before rushing to confirm the *de facto* existence of George W. Bush. We need to define our terms more explicitly. Do we mean the Bush who promised to unite the country by listening to Democrats and Republicans alike? Or the Bush who used the Patriot Act to dismantle America's Constitutional freedoms? Do we mean the president who holds human life so sacred that he wants to prohibit doctor-assisted suicide? Or the president who has endorsed the death penalty throughout his political career? All of these diverse … *personae*, shall we say, make it hard for us to pinpoint precisely what we mean by "Bush."

Perhaps a more instructive way to approach the enigma of George W. Bush is to examine broader symbolic archetypes. To this end, I have constructed three paradigms, known as "Myth," "Monster," and "Marionette," which may prove useful in categorizing the level of existence of our 43rd president.

The "Myth" Paradigm is perhaps the simplest place to start. To satisfy this paradigm, we must show either that George W. Bush does not exist, or – at the very least – that those words or actions attributed to him lack an essential credibility. Reports of his evasiveness and self-contradiction are encouraging in this regard, as are the excuses and justifications offered by his supporters. Even the notion that aliens stole Bush's brain gives him, shall we say, a certain larger-than-life quality characteristic of mythological figures. The same holds true for the impressive data presented here today on pop-culture iconology.

Yet the "Myth" Paradigm does not fully satisfy the evidence as we know it. Bush's economic, military, and civil rights policies hardly measure up to the storied feats of folklore heroes. His words, too, as we saw earlier, often lack a certain heroic stamp. And then there's the requirement of a heroic or "tragic" flaw. Supporters of the "Myth" Paradigm are quick to point out that George W. Bush is hardly lacking in this regard. Unfortunately, there seems to be widespread disagreement as to exactly *which* of his flaws merits strongest consideration. The hubris of the Iraq invasion; the greed of corporate pandering; the fiscal profligacy of his tax cuts; the disregard for civil liberties: these are but a few of the tragic flaws that, taken alone, could each have satisfied the "Myth" Paradigm admirably, but together may push us inexorably closer to the "Monster" Paradigm instead.

Webster's Dictionary defines a "monster" as "… a threatening force … a person of unnatural or extreme wickedness or cruelty." Clearly, the tragic flaws cited above, when viewed in combination, more than fulfill these criteria. However, many noted Bush advocates have suggested that none of this is Bush's fault; that he is, in fact, a victim of circumstance. If verifiable, this could move the existence of George W. Bush within the purview of our third paradigm: that of "Marionette."

The "Marionette" Paradigm is, in some ways, the hardest to define. Obviously, it must include any situation where George W. Bush's words and deeds are under the direct control of another person. We've heard of the machinations of Karl Rove, and the infamous "debate prompter" bulging beneath the suit jacket. Less clear-cut, perhaps, are those instances of group manipulation by special-interest lobbies: the neo-Conservatives, the Evangelical Christians, the corporate PACs, and so on. Arguably, such cases still meet the fundamental "Marionette" criteria. More towards the fringes of the "Marionette" Paradigm, however, is the theory that George W. Bush has been "tempest-tossed" – to put it dramatically – by circumstances beyond his control. The alien brain theft; the Büshler impersonation plot; the excuse that "God told him to do it"; the mental affliction which compels him to make such Freudian slips as: "Saddam would still be in power if he were the president of the United States, and the world would be a lot better off": these are all certainly indicators of outside control of one form or another. Yet their very bizarreness gives them an *outré* quality which would seem to shift them closer to the "Myth" paradigm than the "Marionette." We have come full circle.

So ... George W. Bush: "Myth," "Monster," or "Marionette"? The debate continues, and we may never reach a definitive answer. We must persevere, however, in piecing together anecdotal evidence regarding the existence of George W. Bush, if we hope to achieve a breakthrough in time for next year's symposium. We've made an impressive start. We must not let the trail grow cold. As George W. Bush himself purportedly advocated on May 7, 2002: "One of the things we've got to make sure that we do is anything." We owe it to future historians, as well as to ourselves, to heed this sage advice.

Thank you all very much for coming. Good night, and I hope to see all of you here again next year.

About the Author

Douglas Watson was born in the U.S. and raised in England, and enjoys the nationalities of both countries. After earning his Bachelor's and Master's degrees from Oxford University, he moved to Portland, Oregon, where he divides his time between teaching and writing. In addition to his novels, he is the author of several plays, which have been produced in Portland, Seattle, and elsewhere. He has one daughter, Kimberley.

About the Illustrator

Lynn Pass majored in art education at Indiana University, and received her Master's degree from Ohio State. She teaches art at a high school near Portland, Oregon, and loves working with her creative and talented art students. Favorite media include painting and fused glass, for which she is often inspired by the beautiful flora and fauna of the Pacific Northwest. She greatly appreciates the support she gets from her husband and her two grown daughters.